KINDNESS MATTERS:
Hospitality in a Hostile World

KINDNESS MATTERS

HOSPITALITY
IN A
HOSTILE WORLD

Rev. Dale Fushek
and
Jody Serey

ISBN: 978-1-881276-19-7

Web site: www.kindnessmattersbook.com

TABLE OF CONTENTS

KINDNESS MATTERS: HOSPITALITY IN A HOSTILE WORLD

INTRODUCTION

Why write about hospitality? In a world full of problems, run-away technologies, and violence, why focus on something as basic as hospitality? The answer is twofold: (1) We believe that hospitality, like kindness, really does matter; and (2) we believe that hospitality is becoming a lost art.

All of us know something about hospitality. We remember the smell of our Italian grandmother's spaghetti sauce on Sunday afternoon. We recall the pink bakery boxes with the white string that cluttered the kitchen counter in the homes of our Polish aunts. And on a deeper level, some of us remember the images of Mother Teresa of Calcutta carrying a dying person into her home to care for him. And for sure, these smells and sights speak of hospitality. But in our often hostile world, our culture is getting worse at understanding and living out a true sense of welcoming. Despite the best efforts of Martha Stewart, sincere hospitality is getting more difficult to live. What Martha Stewart and the folks at HGTV and the food network are teaching us is the art of entertaining, not welcoming.

We have written this book to encourage ourselves and others to take a fresh look at how well we are doing being true hosts. Every person, family, ministry, business, and church community needs to evaluate their efforts honestly and not simply presume they are receiving an "A" for "awesome" when it comes to anticipating the needs of others. Read, reflect, re-evaluate, and re-commit to turning our world of hostility into a world with a new spirit and understanding of hospitality.

We welcome you to **Kindness Matters** and we hope that what we share in this book, and the discussion it may provoke, will matter to you and your family.

May the world be a better place because we have welcomed each other into our hearts.

Rev. Dale Fushek

Jody Serey

CHAPTER 1
WHAT IS HOSPITALITY?

REV. DALE FUSHEK - JODY SEREY

REV. DALE FUSHEK

As you begin to read this, you may be surprised by the topic we have chosen. After all, hospitality is simple. Just be nice to people who come to your home or work. What is the big deal? But the truth is, hospitality is much deeper and richer than being NICE. It is a gift to the person who receives it, and to the person who shows it.

The root of the word hospitality is the word "host." Other familiar words such as "hospital" and "hospice" are derived from the same root. A hospital is a place where sick people are hosted. A hospice is a place where dying people are hosted. In other words, hospitals and hospices are places where people offer their specific services and medical training to those who are in need. But real hospitality is not just HOSTING. Real hospitality is about anticipating the need of another person and having a willingness to meet that person's need. A hospital anticipates the need a sick person has for surgery, medicine, and healing. A hospice anticipates the need for pain control and a peaceful environment for someone who is preparing to enter eternity.

Besides the industries of the sick, we are all familiar with the term "hospitality industry." It is a major force that drives many local economies. In fact, numerous schools and universities offer certifications and degrees in hospitality. Airports, hotels, vacation destinations, theme parks, and restaurants specialize in anticipating needs. Airports have small kiosks or stores ready to sell two-ounce bottles of mouthwash and shampoo to travelers who need to comply with new carry-on regulations. Hotels make sure they are ready to sell you snacks in case you are hungry when you arrive in their lobbies. Amusement parks rent strollers. Restaurants have kid friendly menus. The hospitality industry is huge and profitable. The hospitality industry is happy to make arrangements for conferences and conventions. Meals, coffee bars and meeting rooms are readily available for the right amount of money. Nationally and internationally, the hospitality industry thrives.

It is interesting that the industry utilizes a common term, "barriers to entry". Studies are frequently done which examine all sorts of "barriers" that would make something appear inhospitable. Costs, locations, employee attitudes, traffic flow, and the new concept of being "user-friendly" are studied in great detail. In the hospitality industry anything which appears to be unwelcoming turns into a lack of profitability. If tolerated for any period of time, unwelcoming elements can soon turn into economic bankruptcy.

There is nothing intrinsically wrong or bad about the hospitality industry. People trained to anticipate and provide needs and wants of travelers and convention goers can provide great service. Vacations create amazing memories that bond families. Conventions bring people together to learn and grow. But, the basis of real hospitality is not profit. It is human dignity.

There are many places in scripture where hospitality is shown and taught. For Christians, the story of the Good Samaritan is a classic example. In Luke (10:25-37), Jesus teaches his followers how to be a good neighbor. It is the unlikely person, a Samaritan, who anticipates the needs of a man who has been robbed, beaten, and left for dead on the side of the road. With compassion the Samaritan binds the man's wounds and takes him to the innkeeper. He gives the innkeeper instructions and money that anticipate and meet the hurting man's needs. Jesus instructs his followers to go and do the same as the Samaritan man.

There are many other examples in the New Testament of hospitality. The story of the Prodigal Son is about the amazing hospitality of the father in welcoming home his wayward son. The story of Mary and Martha is a true teaching on hospitality. Martha is anxious and worried about the housekeeping details of hospitality and pays no attention to Christ. Christ unaffirms the details of hospitality and reaffirms the focus on him as the person. Even the story of the woman caught in adultery is a story of the inhospitality of those who judge her and the incredible hospitality of Jesus in welcoming her into his mercy.

There are also many specific quotes regarding hospitality in the New Testament. Paul says in his letter to the Hebrews (13:1-2) "Let brotherly love continue. Do not neglect to show hospitality to strangers, for thereby some have entertained angels."

1Timothy tells church leaders they must be "sober-minded, self-controlled, respectable and hospitable." In his first letter Peter (4:9) says, "Show hospitality to one another without grumbling."

The Lord himself is quoted in St. Matthew's gospel (23:35) saying that hospitality will be a basis for eternal judgment. "For I was hungry and you gave me food, I was thirsty and you gave me drink, I was a stranger and you welcomed me."

The basic principle of hospitality is human dignity. Whether you are a humanist, a Christian, or a person of faith in almost any belief system, the human person is viewed as an entity deserving respect. Within faith communities, the human person is often seen as the incarnation of God or a being in which God dwells in a unique way. In humanistic systems, the human being is elevated because the human is good, so good, that God is not even seen as necessary. In almost all principled systems, the human being is seen as part of a community of persons and the communal nature of humanity gives rise to even greater status. The common good is upheld as the greatest good, and treatment of the common good is often the basis for judging between good and evil.

Human dignity is not based upon an individual's choices or behavior. Human dignity is a status which gives every living human – young or old, sick or well, rich or poor – the right to freedom, justice, and respect.

Hospitality in its essence springs forth from an understanding of human dignity. Welcoming another, caring for the needs of another, and anticipating the needs of another are ways that principled people live. Seeing another through eyes that are not clouded by fear, disgust, prejudice, or selfishness is a goal we all should seek.

To be a hospitable person means to anticipate the needs of the person or persons who will cross your path. When they do, the hospitable person LISTENS and RESPONDS. Hospitality is not necessarily an action as much as it is an attitude. It allows another into your space, your heart, your life. The other may come with a simple need: to be recognized, called by name, or directed towards restroom facilities. The other may come with a need for food, water, or a door large enough to accommodate a wheel chair. The need may be more complex: counseling, addiction therapy, a place to stay, or job training. But, whatever the need is, the greeting is the same: "welcome."

It is easy to understand why hospitality can be difficult. And is hard to understand why an entire industry is willing to do it for profit, but so many churches are unwilling to offer it in order to appear like they are spiritually elite and "upscale."

One of the great spiritual writers of our times is Henri Nouwen. He has addressed the issue of hospitality as a core issue of humanity and spirituality. In his book **Reaching Out**, Nouwen says "If there is any concept worth restoring to its original depth and evocative potential it is the concept of hospitality. It is one of the richest biblical terms that can deepen and broaden our insight in our relationships to our fellow human beings. Old and New Testament stories not only show how serious our obligation is to welcome the stranger in our home, but they also tell us that guests are carrying precious gifts with them, which they are eager to reveal to a receptive host. When hostility is converted into hospitality then fearful strangers can become guests revealing to their hosts the promise they are carrying with them. Then in fact, the distinction between host and guest proves to be artificial and evaporates in the recognition of the new found unity."

JODY SEREY

"Hi! My name is John, and I'll be taking care of you tonight."

This familiar greeting has become an integral part of the American restaurant experience, and is usually accompanied by wait staff members, a flurry of menus, and an explanation of the evening's specials.

What we usually interpret this introduction to mean is, "My name is John, and while you are here I will try to accommodate your lactose intolerance and your peanut allergy, and I will also mop up spilled water and replace napkins that are dropped on the floor. You, in turn, will leave me a small financial token of your feigned appreciation for a brief period of servitude that is part of the contemporary form of slavery that I am trying to endure while I put myself through school. And the poached salmon is especially good tonight."

However, in another era, "I'll be taking care of you" meant exactly that. Your host took over responsibility in total for your comfort, physical safety, and defense of reputation because you were his guest. It was a pattern of social functioning that was ancient, powerful, and not subject to change. It was simply how things were done.

We have all experienced what hospitality is not. Most of us can conjure up a memory of a time and place where we most definitely were not welcome. No matter how many years may have passed since we were rebuffed, ignored, or even ejected from a location – the scene still hurts when we relive it.

Time does not heal all wounds. We all remember something we would prefer to forget, if we only could.

Were you the new kid at school, and when you tried to sit at a table in the lunchroom that first day you were told you weren't wanted? Did you accept a job at a company, and discover that the other employees resented your arrival?

Did you marry into a family and find yourself at a Thanksgiving dinner seated by relatives who did not approve of your profession, politics, skin color, religious background, level of education, country of origin, or the football team you were cheering for? Or, maybe you were the stepson at the table of a family whose name was different than your own, and whose stories and anecdotes were not part of the memories of the family that you still carried in your own heart?

Possessions often dictate whether we are welcomed or not into a room, community, or gathering. Have you ever put your keys into the palm of a smirking valet at a fancy hotel when you went to park your modest family car while you attended a wedding reception or an office Christmas party? Were you ever given the stink eye by a clerk in an upscale department store because you were the "wrong" age or shape for the brands being sold inside?

Have you ever tried to order a sandwich at a fast food restaurant when the cooks and counter help just want to punch out and go home? Have you sat in an emergency room with a toddler who had put beans up his nose, and you knew the doctor on call thought you were a terrible parent, and your kid deserved every lima that had disappeared into a dark nasal cavity?

Were you ever a prisoner of war, a battered partner or spouse, or an abused child? Do you feel ostracized from the embrace of a community because of a physical disability, an intellectually disabled child, an old quarrel, a new accusation, or a lack of monetary resources?

From small bruises to gaping wounds, a lack of hospitality is hurtful and potentially permanently damaging.

So now that we have glanced at what it isn't, let us consider what hospitality can be. A broad, general definition of its essence is the friendly reception of guests and strangers. "Guests and strangers" – in other words, ones we know, and ones we don't know. And that would include everybody in our entire existence, wouldn't it? When you encounter another person, you either know him or her, or you are meeting for the first time.

In fact, the word hospitality is from the Latin "hospes," which means host, guest, or stranger. So it is a term that encompasses every face we encounter, including the one in the mirror.

To the ancient Greeks, hospitality was a divine right. A host was compelled to make sure his guest's needs were met. A person's social standing and status in the community hinged largely on his ability to be a good host.

The early Celts defined hospitality more from a perspective of sanctuary than of etiquette or entertainment. Celtic tradition not only demanded that a guest be brought in close to the fire and given food and shelter, but that he be protected from enemies and come to no harm while under somebody else's care.

In India, "the guest is God." In many traditional stories, a stranger or guest arrives to share a meal or to seek shelter, and it is eventually revealed that the stranger at the table is literally a god in disguise who has stepped over the threshold and entered a home.

In the time that Jesus of Nazareth was born, the requirements of hospitality were exact, and applied to all members of the community – not just to strangers and guests. Hospitality mandated that a host offer food, water, shelter and protection. However, a host was also required to protect guests from displays of disrespect, verbal attack, embarrassment or dishonor at the hands of other guests. Conversely, guests were expected to conduct themselves in a manner that refrained from insulting or demeaning other guests or their host, and to never abuse the hospitality of the host. And perhaps most significantly, it was assumed that a current guest would be willing to act as a host for others in the future, especially for the one who had taken them in and cared for them in the past. These traditions were at the heart of how the members of the community interacted with each other, and protected each other from poverty and marginalization.

Throughout human history, the act of sharing food has suggested a level of trust and acceptance between the ones eating a meal together. It is not just the act of receiving food that is most significant (after all, prison guards usually provide enough rations for prisoners to survive).

It is the action of "dipping into the same bowl" that defines the relationship between host and guest. The gesture that elevated even the most esoteric of rituals of hospitality to an act of genuine affection was that of the host dipping a select piece of bread into the bowl, and offering it to a guest. If the offering was accepted by the guest from the hand of the host, the wordless pact between them was powerful. And if the host was later betrayed by the one he had honored, the betrayal seemed even more bitter.

Hospitality is a relationship, a true dynamic. In scientific terms, an inhospitable environment – one that is not conducive to the sustaining of life – is often marked by extreme cold or heat, a lack of water and oxygen, and the absence of any source of sustenance or nourishment. However, in the confines of this definition there is no deliberate malice involved, and this distinction is enormous when compared to what happens when hospitality is absent in human interaction.

In human terms, an environment lacking warmth and welcome, respect for human dignity, and tolerance for diversity can also be a wasteland in terms of viable relationships. Today, we hear and say much about the phenomenon of bullying. A true plague from playgrounds to corporate boardrooms, bullying occurs when a person or group repeatedly attempts to harm someone who is weaker, or is perceived to be weaker. It is a pattern of deliberate harm and humiliation, and is perpetuated because of the satisfaction it brings to the bully because of the sense of power it delivers.

Bullying can be as subtle as shunning the girl with developmental disabilities or the neighbor whose religious head covering is conspicuous in a community of licensed logo baseball caps. However, it can be as toxic and violent as the relentless harassment of a high school student to the point of suicide, or the destruction online of a former friend's or colleague's personal or professional reputation. Bullying is the antithesis of hospitality.

Hospitality is unrequested sanctuary extended by a host. It

goes far beyond cute little soaps in the powder room. It is a reflex, an instinct, and a philosophy based in everything that is "home." However, it is even more than that.

Robert Frost's powerful poem, "The Death of the Hired Man," tells of Silas, an old and dying farm laborer who returns to the place where he'd worked, and that he'd left long before. Mary, the farmer's wife, defends Silas' return by saying, "Home is the place where, when you have to go there / They have to take you in. / I should have called it/ Something you somehow haven't to deserve."

Hospitality is not just being allowed to enter a place and call it home, whether for the first or the last time. Hospitality is what is offered in anticipation of another's needs, before a request has to be made, before a plea has to be issued – and before a handout is ever necessary.

CHAPTER 2
HOW DID WE BECOME
AN INHOSPITABLE SOCIETY?

JODY SEREY

A quick trip to any big box home and garden store provides lots of purchasing options for the devout Antihost. There is a sign to post by the button to the doorbell that says "No Soliciting." This assumes that the person at the door will have made it past the "Beware of Dog" sign to stand on the doormat that commands "Go Away!"

However, my personal favorite says, "Come back with a warrant."

There are many theories as to how we have become a nation of bolts, locks, alarms, unlisted numbers, gated communities, secret codes, and PINs. Sociologists, behavioral psychologists, anthropologists, theologians, philosophers, and talk show hosts all have opinions as to why humans visit on other human beings everything from basic rudeness to outright mayhem. Although few would argue that there is a marked difference from being snubbed at an office party to being felled in an unprovoked attack with a hatchet – the fabric of the negative behavior is woven with a common thread: a lack of empathy.

What is empathy? Quite simply, it is the ability to understand and share someone else's feelings. The adage that is most often seen on posters and plaques is, "Don't judge another until you have walked a mile in his shoes."

It's not as easy as it sounds, despite the fact that we appear to be hardwired for better behavior than we often display. Yet some have suggested that a natural suspicion exists in all animals towards species not like their own. Ostensibly, this aversion to what is different – what is "other" – is part of a deeper instinct to ensure an animal's survival, and maintain the strength of a species.

Regardless of the debate, empathy is an abstract quality that seems to be innate in most human beings, and appears in the behavior of many primates. But to know that right now there are chimps that are acting with more compassion than some of us are isn't exactly reassuring – especially to employers, or parents of adolescent children.

The first signs of what we identify as human empathy appear in babies almost from birth. Newborns in a nursery will all break into a chorus of wailing when one baby starts to cry – to the regret of the nursing staff on duty. A very young child barely past a first birthday will attempt to help an adult who is struggling to do something like reach for an object.

But like language, the development of the inherent quality of empathy can be stunted if it isn't fostered early in a child's development. In fact, ancient societies that raised boy children to be warriors deliberately exposed them to conditions of unrelenting brutality to strip away anything resembling mercy and sympathy, and to replace these attributes with carefully honed cruelty and ruthlessness. They were conditioned to win in battle, regardless of what happened to them, or the ones around them. Nothing else mattered, or was allowed to exist. Mothers told their sons, "Come home with your shield, or on it."

We often speak of the resilience of children, and how they seem to be able to survive horrendous conditions and abuse with astonishing success. However, there are many studies that trace aggression and bullying to trauma early in age. And the prison population is loaded with individuals whose lack of ability to empathize with other people created both criminals and the victims they preyed upon.

Assuming that inhospitality can also be attributed, at least in part, to a lack of empathy – what are more common manifestations of its (inhospitality's) presence in our daily lives?

Betrayal, large and small, is a form of inhospitality. A failure to keep a commitment or a promise (a vow, a secret, a contract, an understanding), betrayal can only occur when one party has assumed that the other party was sincere and/ or trustworthy.

When trust is shattered, it is often difficult to re-establish, because of the fear of being betrayed again. And sadly, trust can only exist to the extent that fear is absent.

Inhospitality appears as our view of "other." We speak in euphemistic terms of the "right" people and the "wrong" people, the "right" side of the tracks and the "wrong "side of the tracks, and the "right" influences and the "wrong" influences.

Reality shows foster a general acceptance of inhospitality in the form of scathing judges whose bad manners and contempt for the ones whose dancing, singing, fashion design, or cupcakes are being scrutinized and criticized (usually without anything resembling genuine constructive commentary) on national television. What may seem like frothy entertainment may be desensitizing our television viewing population to the very real pain caused to very real people by the lack of empathy of thumbs-down judges calling for the virtual deaths of contestants for the amusement of the crowd. Roman gladiators aren't so far removed from our current diversions.

The conflict between Cain and Abel was based on differing methods of making a livelihood, which in turn led to different offerings being made to God, only one of which was shown favor. The angry sibling rivalry that resulted was deadly. (It is somewhat sobering to realize that today Adam's and Eve's family would be termed "dysfunctional" and Cain would be said to have had "anger management problems.")

We have all seen what labeling a group, promoting stereotypes, making jokes and slurs, exhibiting negative body language to a newcomer, and ignoring somebody can do. The middle school years represent the Dark Ages for many people who may have become successful by society's standards later on – but who never lose their memory of misery on the sidelines.

The ideology of "otherness" has spawned some of our human society's worst activities: slavery; child abuse; domestic violence; marginalizing of the handicapped, mentally ill, and socially unconventional; sexism; racism; class discrimination; religious persecution, and other regrettable detours from all that we are capable of being. Prejudice is the collective denial of acceptance of an entire group of people through a shared attitude of inhospitality by another group of people. It is insidious because it masquerades as good taste, refinement, superiority, an educated view, and (irony of ironies) a true understanding of "how things really are."

We have myriad ways today to facilitate communication; Facebook, Twitter, Skype, and other means to access each other should provide us with ways to stay truly connected despite distance and circumstance.

However, quite often listening and comprehending seem to be taking a back seat to what is defined by some sociologists as "social media narcissism," especially concerning individuals who maintain a sizeable presence online. Some have speculated that by maintaining an enormous base of "friends" or "likes," it is possible to elicit apparent approval from enough of the online crowd at any given time to create the appearance of approval, and "right behavior."

Frequently, empathy is not emphasized. Discernment is not required. Compassion is not rewarded. And if conditions are right and the "audience" morphs into a chanting mob encouraging even more and more selfish or outrageous displays – can virtual bullying and the most extreme forms of inhospitality be all that far removed from the realm of possible outcomes?

Recently, a new social media app was released, created specifically for those who hate social media, and the human race. Called "Hell Is Other People," it is advertised as an experiment in anti-social media that calculates safe zones around a city where people can feel certain they'll avoid encountering anyone they know. It's sad to report that sales are brisk.

CHAPTER 3
HOSPITALITY AS A
BASIS FOR RELIGION

REV. DALE FUSHEK

Many churches are in trouble today. Even though Americans are a deeply religious people, and hang on to their traditional religion, churches are hemorrhaging members, commitment, and money. The question that looms over houses of worship is, "What is the future of institutional religion in the United States?"

To begin to answer this question, we first have to ask the deeper question, "What is the purpose of religion?" The word "religion" itself means to "bind back." So, in a sense, religion is supposed to bind us back to God, to our core values, and our beliefs. But, in reality, the business of religion is so huge that institutions take on lives of their own. And for many religions, their purpose seems to be self-perpetuation and survival.

Religion should be a way of life that helps an individual and a community to get in touch with God. Religion should not try to create God, control God, limit God, or contain God. It should reflect God in His greatness, His love, and His mercy. Religion should make the God of scripture come alive in a contemporary world.

Within Christianity we believe in a Triune God, that is the Trinity. To simply explain the Trinity (which of course is impossible), God is love and in order to love there must be one who is loved. The Father and the Son are the Lover and the Beloved. The Spirit is the energy or the bond of love (theologians call it the "spiration") between the first two persons of the Trinity. The Triune God is perfect in every way.

The perfect God then creates an imperfect world. He creates the stars and the galaxy that at times collide with each other. He creates the wind that sometimes turns into a damaging tornado. And He creates humans, who are gifted with free will and the ability to choose love or act against it.

The Trinity then invites humans into a relationship. The relationship we are invited into is a permanent one which we call heaven. In other words, the perfect God is the perfect Host for all of eternity. God is hospitality and throughout scripture we see a God who welcomes both sinners and saints.

We as humans often struggle with God. We feel unworthy and many of us spend a life time learning how to welcome the hospitable God into our hearts and our lives. Even though God loves us and always welcomes us into His life, we seem to reject His invitation to be loved.

Religious groups are meant to reflect the hospitality of God. God who is the perfect and almighty Welcome should be preached from the pulpit and imitated in the practice of religion. Yet, what often happens is that many religious bodies take on the culture of a country club instead of the culture of God. Religions become concerned with making sure that membership has its privileges and the Word and the sacraments are limited to those they deem worthy. Churches become concerned with deciding who is and who is not saved. They have become like the Pharisees in placing emphasis on rules, regulations, and rituals instead of relationships.

Churches are in a tough spot. They are businesses and must pay the bills. They must do something to maintain customer loyalty. Yet at the same time, in order to do so, they are rejecting the one thing they are called to do, and that is to reflect God.

The spiritual life should be about hospitality. It is the journey of accepting and welcoming God into our daily lives. It is also learning to accept a love, a warmth that is freely given to us. But, the spiritual life does not stop there. The spiritual life is all about learning to be an instrument of hospitality and warmth for one another. To summarize it: the spiritual life is welcoming the already present God into our consciousness and then sharing His welcome with our brothers and sisters by welcoming them into our lives.

Therefore, religion should be the body of people who are committed to reflecting the hospitality of God. When a church denies a sinner entrance into the temple, the church itself becomes sinful. When a church begins to deny someone sacraments because of a superficially created teaching, the church puts itself at risk of being included among the Pharisees. The church is not a place, like an exclusive country club, that is intended to make a few feel chosen and selected by keeping others out. A church which determines the qualifications inherent in the categories of the sinners and the saved is encouraging its own members to reject true humility and they are encouraging their believers to enter a world of idolatry. When you lose humility, you will always lose hospitality. When you lose hospitality, you lose God. When you lose God, you've lost everything that matters, and religion has no reason to exist.

I recently read a sermon by a well-known Christian pastor, A.W. Tozer. He said something which literally shook me to the core. Tozer said, "This is my finding: there is nothing that Jesus has ever done for any of His disciples that He will not do for any other of His disciples." (Hey – that's you and me!)

If this is true (and I sincerely believe it is), it is mind-blowing. What Jesus did for the woman caught in adultery, He is willing to do for you and me. What Jesus did for the blind man, He is willing to do for you and me. What He did for His apostles, He is willing to do for you and me.

Where are the churches? Why aren't they screaming this message from the rooftops? Why isn't the amazing hospitality of God being preached to those who are lost? Why isn't it preached to those who come to church each Sunday?

Many of our churches hunker down behind the closed doors of their buildings –buildings which appear to have been built to resemble a fortress, a palace, or a bank. Why is there so much energy expended in religion to keep out those who disagree or those that have lost their way? Why do church leaders stay hidden behind their robes while they judge who does and who doesn't have a chance at salvation? And who are they to assume the role that rightfully belongs to God?

The essence of religion must be hospitality. Welcome. Welcome to the word of God. Welcome to the world of grace. Welcome to the sacraments. Welcome to community. Welcome to mercy. Welcome to eternal life.

Communities need to be re-educated. Church leaders must become re-directed. "Welcome" needs to become the battle cry of all Christians.

Churches are complex, convoluted places these days. The healthy and the sick sit together to hear the same sermon. People are busy, stressed, worried, and have many needs. Church communities and leaders are stressed as well, with financial shortfalls, limited staff, and often overwhelming demands. But the results of all these challenges and demands cannot lead the church to turns its back on its most essential mission – welcoming others to share in the life of God.

In his book titled **The Gospel of Inclusion**, Bishop Carlton Pearson describes his belief that a new movement is forming within Christianity. He believes that some people finally comprehend the real gospel message regarding the radical love of God which is intended for all. Pearson says (pg. 275) "There are probably more disenchanted Christians in the world than there are faithful ones, not to mention millions of other weary religionists looking for a way out of the rut. Churches and religions have abused people for centuries, and they have much to answer for. This movement will sweep the world; it will not wipe out religion as the fear preachers like to cry, but it could and might end religion as a device to control, steal, and oppress. Christ Consciousness – the understanding that we don't have to convert, just convince people they are loved, by loving them – will grow."

The frozen chosen must die. Religion must become a beacon of hope for those who are seeking as well as those who count themselves among the saved. In practical terms, many changes need to happen. Communities need to be friendlier. Believers need to learn each other's names. Churches need to do a better job preaching a relevant message. Condemnation and judgment need to stop. The poor and the disenfranchised need to be given places at the table. No one should be denied the sacraments. The rules of control need to be dropped.

The message on the church door needs to change from "quiet please" to "all are welcome." And in the midst of it all, the gospel needs to start changing our individual hearts as well as the heart of religion.

The greatest sign of God's hospitality is heaven. We can only imagine what heaven will be like. The vision of the opening of the Pearly Gates and entering to see loved ones gathered with God around a heavenly banquet is very inspiring. Wouldn't it be great to describe entering our churches the same way we describe entering heaven?

Questions to consider:

Let's talk about our community:

If someone walked into our church for the first time, what would they experience?

When you first came to this community, what did you and your family experience?

What is the LEAST welcoming aspect of our community?

What is the MOST welcoming aspect of our community?

What makes our community UNIQUE?

Is our preaching positive and uplifting? Is our preaching negative and downgrading?

Are there any groups that might sense barriers in our church? Youth? Minorities? Divorced? Poor? Deaf? Handicapped? Sinners? Elderly? Gay? Others?

Is our pastor someone who includes others, especially those who might be attending for the first time? Is our congregation open to new people?

Are people free to ask questions, doubt, and think for themselves? Are people in our community FREE to seek God?

Does our church look like hope? Feel like hope? Smell like hope?

Is the Gospel of unconditional love being preached by our community in words and in action?

What changes do we need to make in order for our community to become more welcoming?

What changes do I personally need to make in order to become a more hospitable person?

CHAPTER 4
HOSPITALITY AS A
BASIS FOR BUSINESS

JODY SEREY

Hospitality and business are often paired together --
usually in the context of the hospitality industry, which
may or may not be truly hospitable in its dealings with the
human race. Even when it is not being used to analyze the
migration habits of tourists and visitors, the word "hospitality"
is usually misapplied to the dynamics of marketing and sales.
Projecting an aura of welcome is touted as being an effective
strategy for softening the resistance of a potential customer
and encouraging him or her to relax, and then relax the purse
strings.

Assuming that genuine unconditional hospitality involves
absolute openness to the other, let us consider some actual
instances where the door of commerce slammed shut in the
face of a potential customer.

1. In a prominent ranching family, the wife was the motorhead garage mechanic of the family. When the day came to purchase some new trucks, the husband put the company checkbook into his wife's hands and she drove the family car (which she had serviced herself) into Phoenix with the intent of purchasing a company fleet. It was to be a cash sale for multiple identical vehicles, and the decision about what to buy was hers and hers alone.

At the first dealership, the sales reps ignored her until she interrupted their personal conversation, and then they attempted to steer her towards the SUVs. At the second dealership, she was brushed aside when she said she wanted to look at a truck, so she returned to her car and drove farther down the road. At the third much smaller dealership, the owner – who had been in the auto business a very long time – waved hello and came out to meet her. She told him she needed what information he could give her about a "reliable workhorse truck."

He welcomed her into his dealership and got her a cup of coffee, and made a space for her at a table in his little office. He answered her questions, and generally made her feel welcome and never indicated in the slightest that he thought she might be wasting his time. After a couple of test drives, a lot of phone calls, and some forays onto the Internet – they reached a consensus as to what make and model truck might be best for her. He said to her, "Would you like to take some brochures home so you can do some more thinking?"

She said, "No, you've already been very helpful. So I would like you to order me five of these trucks, all exactly alike."

2. A young war veteran who survived severe injuries that cost him a leg and left him with facial scars discovered that despite the plethora of rules and regulations requiring commercial buildings to be accessible to people with physical disabilities, many places of business aren't easy to navigate. For him, doors are narrow, counters are high and elevators are shared grudgingly with other passengers who read the numbers instead of acknowledging his presence.

He observed that even though he is once again healed and healthy and maneuvers his wheelchair with the skill of a NASCAR driver, he feels "damaged" every time he tries to leave his house to run a simple errand. "I really am doing great, and want to get back to living a completely independent life. But until I can reach the paper towels in a restroom or don't cause a major scene at a fast food restaurant because I want a refill on my iced tea and I can't reach the dispenser – I remain defined as crippled. And that's not how I see myself."

3. The CEO of a high end department store stated that his company did not want to market to anybody who wasn't "cool" and good-looking. He specifically targeted plus-size teenagers as being undesirable customers, and said he wasn't much interested in selling to "geeky kids." He only wanted the "best" people to be seen leaving the rarified atmosphere of his establishment with one of the store's signature bags. Old people were particularly vilified as being unwanted at his cash registers.

In a similar shopping scenario, the middle aged aunt of a bride-to-be went to the local suburban mall to buy a piece of lingerie for her niece's "personal shower." Wanting to do something extra special for the young woman, she ventured into a widely advertised, almost iconic purveyor of extraordinarily high priced under garments. She gasped at the cost for a bit of lace and some strategically placed elastic, but decided that her niece would be thrilled to get something from the store. The aunt found her niece's size, and began to hunt for something to purchase. Before she made it a quarter of the way around the rack, a "customer service associate" hurled herself in front of the older woman like an avenging underwear angel. Looking up and down at the aunt, the clerk sniffed and said, "You won't find anything in here that will fit you. Why don't you try Lane Bryant or Sears?"

4. When the family came through the door, a medical office staff assumed that the mother with several multi-racial children in tow was "just another one of those mothers" from "that part of town." They herded the family onto the side of the divided waiting area usually reserved for patients with an active communicable illness, and they glared meaningfully at a couple of the children who were restless and somewhat agitated.

It wasn't until the paperwork had been completed and all the identification information presented that it became known that the mother was actually a foster parent specially trained and licensed to care for children with very special needs. She had brought in several of the kids for a series of evaluations for conditions that she identified and was hoping to get treated.

And then there's banking…

The banking industry is viewed by many these days as being a toxic entity that has threatened the well-being of the modern fiscal world. Thomas F. Franklin, a Chicago-area veteran of the commercial banking and financial services industry (www.franklinleadership.com), has devoted much thought to the topic of business ethics, and where they begin. He said recently, "Ethical banking is not an oxymoron."

When asked to comment about the role of hospitality in business, he responded: "Managing hospitality from the top down creates a more ethical environment. Ethical leadership's primary responsibility is the development, communication and refinement of policies, company standards, recruiting, development and sanctioned organizational behavior that is managed through hospitality to create a positive physical, mental, emotional and psychological environment for clients. This sanctioned organizational activity acknowledges that hospitality is not absolute or static in nature.

"It is only accomplished by people that demonstrate a true service perspective defined by the company's mission at all levels of management. The hierarchies of knowledge and information within hospitality must be understood by one who leads the development and implementation of an organization's strategy. From the practical realities found within the management of ethics and integrity in business, leadership establishes and communicates that which is legal as the goal, the target or the standard for people to follow.

"The setting of the standard of being legal as applied to hospitality is important to understand as a goal but not the company's focus. The least of your clients should be treated as you would want to be treated."

The exchange of some kind of currency for goods and services is an activity almost as old as the human race. Indeed, it is an activity that appears to be a part of the interaction of other species, including birds and animals. Stories are told of ravens trading shiny objects for items, of monkeys trading food (one thinks of kids trading lunches on a playground), and of social transactions in the animal kingdom being consummated with "payment."

1 Timothy 6:10 says, "For the love of money is a root of all sorts of evil, and some by longing for it have wandered away from the faith and pierced themselves with many griefs." (Please note that this reading does not say that money is to blame for human suffering. Money is a neutral entity, a mere means to an end. It is the love of it and what it can symbolize that is the catalyst for problems.)

However, when hospitality gets factored out of the equation, the sum total of a business transaction of any kind may not be a mutually beneficial arrangement between two human parties. We can't speak for ravens and monkeys, but they don't seem to sue each other very often in civil court.

In his poem "The Rock," T.S. Eliot asked:

When the Stranger says: "What is the meaning of this city?
Do you huddle close together because you love each other?"
What will you answer? "We all dwell together
To make money from each other"? or "This is a community"?

What would you answer?

CHAPTER 5
HOSPITALITY AS A BASIS FOR LEADERSHIP

REV. DALE FUSHEK

What is leadership? In one of his books, **Prince Caspian**, C.S. Lewis describes a situation in which his fantasy characters are heading back to Narnia. On their route they encounter many dangers. At one point, they meet a lion. Lewis says, "Lucy had her eyes on the lion, and the rest had their eyes on Lucy."

In a real sense, that is a great description of a leader. When the lion approaches (and there are many different lions out there), where do eyes look?

A lot of characteristics are used to describe leaders. Here are a few: good communication skills, ability to motivate, courage, experience, knowledge, integrity, responsibility, focus, flexibility, clarity of purpose, accountability, and self-awareness. I would like to add another characteristic to the list: hospitality, that is, the art of anticipating and providing for the needs of others.

In talking about leadership we can assign leaders into two categories: (1) power leaders and (2) servant leaders. Power leaders are motivated by what they want, what serves their purpose, and what they can gain by having a position of authority. Servant leaders are motivated by hospitality, knowing what are the legitimate needs of others and how we can respond. Servant leaders have a great gift of being able to see the bigger picture, and they understand what the pronoun "US" means in a critical situation.

Throughout recorded history there have been many great leaders. A list could easily include Abraham Lincoln, Winston Churchill, and Martin Luther King, Jr. to name just a few. There have also been great spiritual leaders including Mother Teresa of Calcutta, Archbishop Desmond Tutu and Rev. Billy Graham. And even though each of these folks lived in different situations and different times, they shared the common trait that the eyes of others would be drawn to them in difficult times to find hope, survival, and direction.

Leadership, of course, is needed on every level. Wherever two or more are gathered, some type of leadership is demanded. Leadership exists in politics, business, education, religion, and in families. And in each of these areas, it is possible to have power leaders or servant leaders.

In our contemporary setting, there is a crisis in leadership in at least two key areas: politics and religion. In the political world there are few who are willing to put aside party and personal gain in favor of hospitality. To quote Charlie Sheen, "winning" is the goal. Politicians often do not want to welcome others into the process. They do not listen to others, and they do not care about those who have become marginalized. Excluding others who think differently is considered a virtue by many successful politicians. The result is a system that is congested and constipated.

Unfortunately, religion is no different. And to be honest, in many cases is even worse. Most of us, deep down in our souls, want to believe religious leaders are in it for the right reasons. However, many bishops and pastors simply are not. Religious leaders sometimes want their view of God, the church, and the world to "win." Churches do not respond to the needs of the contemporary world around them because the world does not conform to the image they have created for organized religion. In fact A.W. Tozer, a well- known self-taught theologian from the 1950s, said "nobody expects a cemetery to do anything but conform…but the church is not a cemetery and we should expect much more from it, because what has been should not be lord to tell us what is, and what is should not be ruler to tell us what will be. God's people are supposed to grow."

And yet, when are eyes are drawn toward spiritual leaders to help with spiritual growth, there is often no substance – only fancy vestments and pointed hats. The people of God are often left disappointed. There is no real leadership.

In reality, whether religion or politics, our eyes can be temporarily drawn to the most bizarre or the loudest. But eyes are soon downcast. True leadership is not born out of being able to scream "look at me." True leadership is born out of a desire to listen and to do what is right.

To be a hospitable leader, in any field, a leader must listen in three ways. First, he/she must listen to others and discern their true needs. Second, a leader must listen to the voice of God within them. This voice will lead them to seek truth and the common good. And third, a leader must go into his or her own heart, on a deeper level, and get beyond the surface. This journey into the heart will open the heart and allow others to be welcomed. Few leaders move to this level. Between the stress of the many demands of leadership, and being scrutinized by a gone-wild media, servant leaders are often destroyed. This opens the door for more and more power leaders to fill the void.

We need servant leaders. Jesus gave the example of the true leader in the Gospel of John as he washed the feet of his disciples. Shortly after that, he went a step further in teaching leadership, when he gave his life on the cross. Families need servant leaders in moms, dads, grandparents, and siblings who welcome, value and cherish each member of their tribe. Businesses need to have bosses and CEOs who anticipate the needs of their customers and their co-workers. Our political system, currently broken by the weight of so many power leaders, cries for true and hospitable leadership. And our churches and our faith communities need men and women who can envision the future and who can listen to the needs of their brothers and sisters who journey with them.

In times of turmoil all eyes turn to leaders. We seem to be in a time of turmoil and confusion, and no one is quite sure where to look. Our country, our families, our schools, our workplaces, and our churches all need people who are willing to listen, to serve, to welcome.

Who will rise from our midst?

CHAPTER 6
HOSPITALITY AS A BASIS FOR POLITICS

JODY SEREY

There are three topics that so-called polite society used to ban altogether from mixed company table conversation: sex, religion, and politics. Etiquette books from the era admonished pursuers of the genteel existence to refrain from discussing these subjects, and to tread softly if "m-o-n-e-y" was mentioned.

After the bitter and acrimonious campaigns that we have endured the past few years – ones that were so vicious that they seemed at times to tear at the very fabric of society – it seems almost laughable to suggest that politics and hospitality could be discussed in tandem. And certainly never, ever during dinner.

So what exactly is the definition of politics? The word is derived from the Greek politicos, meaning "of, for, or relating to citizens." And generally speaking it is the theory and practice of influencing other people on a civic or individual level. There is debate as to whether politics exist among other species of animals, but it seems that we humans are unique in our ability to turn different perspectives and divergent opinions into prolonged armed conflict. Indeed, it seems that the lines are already being drawn for the next presidential election, even before the hatchet wounds from the last one have closed over and quit bleeding.

The dynamics of any two camps going to battle against each other – whether they are entire countries, rival gangs, religious denominations, homeowners associations, school PTA groups, competing corporations, or political parties – are potentially lethal. Brute force quickly replaces sparring, character assassination pushes aside debate, and every blow struck is intended to maim or kill.

We are all familiar with politics leading to misery. William Shakespeare presented Romeo and Juliet as an example of the tragedy that can ensue when issues outstrip any consideration of consequences. The Montagues and the Capulets were temporarily quieted in their plotting against each other after the deaths of the star-crossed teenagers. But even Shakespeare didn't speculate how long the uneasy truce might have lasted.

In the American West during the 1880s to the 1920s, ranchers fought to the death over grazing lands. Sheep were considered invaders, lesser animals than cattle, and were said to ruin grassland by pulling the tender shoots up by the roots when they fed. However, the specific reasons for the animosity between the factions faded in importance as the hatred intensified.

In the hierarchy of animal husbandry that existed, cattlemen (cowboys) were considered to have more prestige than did sheepmen. Therefore, cattlemen had more influence over public officials, and any conflict that ended up in a court of law was usually ruled in the cattlemen's favor. Between 1870 and 1920 when the situation finally simmered down, more than 120 armed confrontations had occurred throughout eight states, 54 men had died, and as many as 100,000 sheep had been slaughtered in raids on flocks.

In Arizona, a feud erupted between two ranch families. A clan of sheep ranchers – the Tewksburys – and a clan of cattle ranchers – the Grahams – escalated their conflict over grazing land, each claiming that the other's animals damaged it and left it useless. The conflict escalated into a war that left as many as 20 people dead, and involved local citizens from all around the area. Killers for hire were involved in the vendetta, and nothing was too underhanded or too violent to be utilized as a strategy.

Gunfights, ambushes, and cold-blooded murder was the legacy left to the memories of the families, who eventually killed each other off to the point that only two men were left standing: Ed Tewksbury and Tom Graham. When Tom Graham died under suspicious circumstances in 1892, Ed Tewksbury was considered the likely suspect. But nothing was ever proven and he was released from custody. He lived until 1904, the only survivor of a deadly rivalry that wiped out two families. In a range war, winning is not only not "everything" – it can cost everything, and amounts to absolutely nothing. Therefore, the next time you find yourself attempting to unravel the rhetoric of verbal combatants, remember that even the way livestock eats grass can become a topic toxic enough to inspire murder.

In the heat of unrestrained political rivalry and aggressive political persecution of any kind, either side may feel completely justified in the severity of their methods to "convince" others that their position is the only one with merit. We have all yawned our way through world history text books that listed wars and mayhem so massive and far-reaching that we found ourselves numbed by their number and description to the point that we detached emotionally from the magnitude of how much suffering has been caused throughout humankind's existence that was the result of politics gone wrong.

So what can be done to introduce a little hospitality to the potential blood bath that has become the business as usual way of politics today? Perhaps the final step is envisioned as being the stepping back from the micro-issues and reaching across the figurative aisle to shake hands over the mutual concerns that are shared by all concerned. But what should be the first step?

Here is a recommendation: nothing. In other words, "don't just do something; stand there."

And listen, listen, listen. Listen to what people are saying, listen to what causes them to raise their voices, or become silent themselves. Hear what they are saying, and don't let the pauses for breath be your cue to jump in with your opinion, viewpoint, or argument.

Share a meal, a bus seat, a bleacher at a ballgame, or an elevator with somebody and assume nothing about their intelligence quotient, the species of their parentage, or the fate of their immortal soul if they appear to differ politically from your views. Welcome the differing perspectives. Preserve the dignity of the individual giving voice to an approach that varies (even drastically) from your own. And do not judge the validity of what others believe, say, or endorse until you can separate opinion from prejudice, fact from bias, and truth from false generalizations.

In both hospitable politics and politics of the common good (however a group or organization defines it), there is ample room for partnering, for coming together for action. One of ironies of shared tragedy – wildfires, tornadoes, floods, acts of terrorism – is that political differences seem to evaporate and diversity ceases to matter for a little while when everybody is concentrating on fixing the something or the somebody that is broken.

Returning to the conventions of polite society – the insistence that certain social protocols be observed can serve a purpose. Manners and etiquette are actually methods of avoiding conflict. However, confusing civility with compatibility is an easy error to make.

In his article for **The Boston Globe** ("Good manners are smart politics," January 17, 2011), former United States senator from New Hampshire, John E. Sununu, wrote: "...I am all for civility. Who isn't? But as America's professional scolds embark upon another 'change the tone' campaign, they should keep a few things in mind.

"**Be careful about longing too wistfully for the civility of yesteryear**. Public discourse marking the civil rights debates of the 1950s and 1960s, the Vietnam-era confrontations of the 1960s and 1970s, and the Iran-Contra and Bork hearings of the 1980s are far from perfect examples of thoughtful moderation. Serious differences in ideology provoke deep emotion. We do today's debates an injustice if we mischaracterize the tone and tenor of those past. **Public figures who blame the media are avoiding their own responsibility**. The media love coarse debate because coarse debate drives ratings and ratings generate profits. Unless the TV producer happens to be William Shakespeare, an argument is more interesting than a soliloquy — and there will never be a shortage of people willing to argue on TV. Politicians wishing to set a better tone should have the discipline to avoid televised cage matches...**Remember the golden rule**. (Not the one about silence — this is politics, after all.) Never — ever — question the motives of your opponent...Questioning a person's motives is a frontal attack on their integrity, implying that they possess some nefarious intention. Too often the cavalier suggestion is corruption — that someone is taking an action in return for special treatment, political payback, or money. Unfortunately, politicians are usually the first to forget that if you assume someone else is acting in bad faith, they will do the same to you. Questioning motives poisons the well. **Lastly, recognize that civility in no way requires an absence of partisanship**."

CHAPTER 7
HOSPITALITY AS A BASIS
FOR PERSONAL RELATIONSHIPS

REV. DALE FUSHEK - JODY SEREY

REV. DALE FUSHEK

The phrase "there are two kinds of people in the world" is way overused. However, I have used it myself while preaching, saying there are "givers and takers."

My nephew recently told me there are two kinds of people in the world – "those who have trucks and those who borrow them."

Let me throw another one out to you. There are two kinds of people in the world – those who "want to intimidate and those who want to be intimate."

The words "intimidate" and "intimate" look like they could come from the same root word. But "intimidate" comes from the word "timid," that is, to make one fearful. The word "intimate" comes from the Latin word "to make known." These two words have meanings that are exactly opposite of each other. And, to be more accurate, perhaps there are not just two different kinds of people. Perhaps each of us has the ability to approach others in two different ways.

Many people try to intimidate others. That is the essence of being a bully. It is also the essence of arrogance, which makes it clear that one person feels that he or she is far above another. Those feelings can be created because of looks, stature, money, power, talent, and perception. They can also arise because of low self-esteem and the need to cover up feelings of inadequacy. Intimidation ultimately is destructive to both the one who is doing the intimidating, and the one who is being intimidated. When intimidation is involved, there is no possibility of a positive interpersonal relationship.

Intimacy, on the other hand, is the foundation on which a human relationship can grow. Intimacy is not about sex; it is about building a bridge between two people who share the human experience. Intimacy involves including another in your conversation and your life. It involves listening to and empathizing with another person. It involves a willingness to trust, to risk, and to communicate.

Intimidation involves no personal strengths. It simply involves demonstrating power, and "acting strong." Intimacy requires genuine strengths such as self-knowledge, self-confidence, and a belief in basic human goodness. When you are truly willing to be intimate you must be strong enough to endure hurt and accept the possibility of being violated.

Intimacy involves hospitality. Welcoming and anticipating

the legitimate needs of another is a sign of maturity and compassion.

Sometimes, people misunderstand hospitality and believe it has to do with being a door mat. However, there is a major difference between being a door mat and a welcome mat. Hospitality is not an excuse for being dysfunctional or an enabler. Bad behavior is simply bad behavior. We do not welcome others into our home or our hearts so they can destroy us. We allow others in so they can experience the unconditional love of God. We give each other the benefit of the doubt. We do not pre-judge or close others out. We do not presume bad behavior or bad intentions, but we do take a risk in every relationship of being hurt or rejected.

On a personal note, I have been through tremendous hurt and rejection in my own life. The church I loved and the community I had given my life to for decades betrayed me. Trusting another person is hard for me. But, relearning how to trust God and what He asks of me are essential parts of being a mature person of faith.

We are often told that love is a deliberate choice – a decision. Hospitality is also a decision. It is a decision to give another the freedom to be who God has called them to be. Hospitality grants another person the freedom to think differently than you do, to feel as they feel, and to become self-actualized. Hospitality listens to the words of others, but also goes deeper by listening to the unspoken words of the heart. Hospitality does not silence another through judgment or anger. It allows a relationship to grow and develop in a natural and healthy way.

Hospitality takes courage. The word "courage" actually comes from the Latin word "cor," which means heart. The core of a person lies in the heart. It takes heart to love, to listen, and to welcome.

Hospitality must begin in our homes. Certainly parents bear the financial burden of maintaining a home, but the responsibility goes far beyond money. It begins with welcoming the spouse. When God blesses a couple with children hospitality includes welcoming each child with their special needs and their unique gifts. It is often assumed that every new member of a family is embraced with joy, but there can be times when circumstances make it difficult to welcome a child into your life.

Children learn from their parents how to welcome their own brothers and sisters. Children must be able to move beyond competing with siblings and learn to value and cherish each other. The family, as a whole, is called to create a welcoming environment for extended family, neighbors, and friends. When children learn the art of hospitality at a young age, it not only enriches their lives, but it can begin to change the world.

Outside the home, in places like schools, children must be given the example of welcoming the new kid and the stranger. Schools often become places of exclusionary cliques. When that happens, someone is always left eating lunch alone. The murders and shootings in schools such as Columbine are extreme examples of what can happen when people feel they are on the outside.

Unfortunately, churches have become places where people

are NOT always welcomed. Individuals who are divorced, gay, are members of minorities, liberals, or conservatives could all tell stories about being unwelcome. A church should be a place where relationships can flourish and grow. God intends for communities to be ONE.

True community is hard work. But the example given in the Acts of the Apostles (Acts 2) reminds us that the early believers welcomed the Holy Spirit and welcomed one another. They devoted themselves to fellowship, and the Lord added to their number "day by day." Perhaps the lack of welcoming the Spirit and each other explains why there is a decline in church attendance. Some surveys suggest that church attendance is down ten percent or more just in the last decade – and overall attendance has been on the decline for years.

Hospitality must become a way of life in our neighborhoods and in our cities. We must choose to trust, to welcome, and to care about others if all of our lives are to become secure. Even the most technologically advanced alarms and security cameras will not save us. Caring about each other and sharing life together can give us the solid ground on which to build a better America, and ultimately a better human race.

There is no doubt that evil exists in our world. There are terrorists, bullies, deranged spirits and lost souls among us. They are never easy to deal with, and are hard to understand. But only in uniting together and welcoming each other will we be able to change our hostile world into a place worthy of the work of God's hands – for that is what we are.

In terms of personal relationships, kindness really does matter.

47

JODY SEREY

I arranged to meet a friend of mine for dinner. She works in an industry that requires constant interaction with the public, and her mood was mixed when she arrived at the little restaurant where we like to get together. She sat down, tossed her purse onto an empty chair, sighed deeply and said, "People. They're just everywhere these days."

Although I laughed at the time, her words come back to me when my own sometimes precarious enchantment with the human race is being thwarted, usually for a seemingly insignificant reason. It seems that many of us are great friends in a crisis, during a "climb every mountain, ford every stream" moment – but not as steadfast as life drags us over the salt flats of everyday sameness.

How many movies have you sat through that incorporated a theme of "quarreling family/couple/friends discover how much they really mean to each other after they survive a natural disaster/alien invasion/disease/economic meltdown/ airplane crash/end of the world as we know it event"?

We dab at our eyes, throw away our popcorn bag, and leave the theater with a new perspective and a rediscovered appreciation of the ones we love. We vow we're never, ever going to take each other for granted again. Nope, no more ingratitude for this bunch. We're in it for the long haul.

We're ready to launch into a chorus of "We Are Family." That is, until we get to the car. Then somebody asks, "Where do you want to go to eat?" And that's when the fight starts.

Personal relationships are so, well, personal. One teeny little promise of 'til death do us part, semper fidelis, or best friends forever, and suddenly it's all so darned serious.

That's only because it is.

Personal relationships are entirely optional. You don't have to participate in them to survive. You can maintain cordial associations – including productive professional alliances – without truly submerging yourself in the clatter and clutter that are created when human beings interact with each other on intimate levels.

So what does hospitality have to do with personal relationships? And isn't there a big difference between sharing a cubicle at the office and sustaining a long-term and intensely complex relationship like marriage?

Of course. But all positive personal relationships include some of the same elements. Tolerance of differences, respect for privacy, consideration, and a big old slam of common courtesy are great for starters. There is also a lot to be said for avoiding keeping another person in a constant state of defensiveness or irritation when it comes to sustaining a long-term association.

More marriages are enfeebled by small, steady transgressions than are blown apart by tragedy. One long-suffering spouse remarked, "I would prefer the direct attack of a dragon. Instead, I am being pecked to death slowly by a single demonic sparrow."

Whether you're making room in your household for the summer for a surly visiting stepchild, trying one more time to show an apathetic co-worker the ins and outs of office

49

procedures, or trying to find some genuine understanding in your heart for a neighbor who just added yet another plastic flamingo to his front yard collection – try to suspend your own feelings, at least temporarily, so there is room in your heart to welcome in the strange along with the stranger. If you can quiet the chorus of resistance in your own head, you may be able to hear the small whisper of explanation as to why people do the things they do. (The stepchild may miss the dog she left back home. The seemly dense coworker may have been up all night caring for a dementia-ravaged parent and is finding it hard to concentrate. The neighbor may be displaying gifts from grandchildren that arrive in the form of pink plastic birds.)

We can name many kinds of welcoming rituals, both formal and simple, that we observe to symbolize to a newcomer (or expected newcomer) that he or she is safe, accepted, and part of a larger whole. Naturalization ceremonies, engagement parties, weddings and commitment rites, ordinations, baby showers, adoption hearings, political candidate meet-and-greets, family reunions, and high school pep rallies all incorporate literal or figurative open arms and unqualified entry into a group. However, the survival rate of the relationships that are recognized symbolically depends on the effort expended by all concerned to acknowledge and honor each other out of reach of the confetti and the sheet cakes.

Positive personal relationships that endure require hospitality that may stumble (we are human, we get tired and forgetful, and we make mistakes), but doesn't stagger off the edge of the cliff of petty bickering and insensitivity. Few things in life are as rewarding as ancient alliances, old friendships, and bonds that are forged for life, one small act of loyalty at a time. It's a lot of work, and it's not for the faint of heart.

However, if you decide that the risks and inconveniences of personal relationships are outweighed by the treasures they can reveal, then buckle up for the long ride, and settle in and pay attention to the scenery along the way.

You don't get a do-over when it comes to a lifetime of relationships, good or bad.

CHAPTER 8
WHAT ARE THE SOLUTIONS FOR INHOSPITABLE CONDITIONS IN SOCIETY

REV. DALE FUSHEK

Pointing a finger at a problem is easy. That's what the prophets in the Old Testament did. They reminded the people of Israel what they were doing to displease their God. The same is true today. The difference is we no longer call them prophets – we call them editorial writers. There are a whole group of people (editorial writers, that is) that actually make a living pointing out what is wrong with our culture and society. And the truth is, no one really expects them to have any solutions to the issues of the day.

So, here we write a whole book about our contemporary problem with hospitality. We can share with you our observations of what is happening in our churches, our businesses, and our neighborhoods. But now, we have to approach the challenge of how to come up with solutions to the problem.

The word "solution" itself is an interesting noun. It comes from the root word meaning "to solve". Another word with the same root (etymology) is the word "dissolve." Actually, dissolve is a great word to associate with the the word solution; that is, how do we make the problem of being an un-hospitable society DISSOLVE?

The easiest thing to do would be to suggest a checklist of ten actions to take. And, as a matter of fact, I will do that. But, the starting point for dissolving this problem isn't practical – it is an abstract concept. You have to start with a change of HEART.

It has been said that no one changes except out of pain. Until a person has been on the outside of hospitality, perhaps no significant change will happen. But maybe, just maybe, if we allow ourselves to see the pain of others, hearts will be changed.

When someone is "left out" or treated rudely, it is natural for that person to ask the simple question "what is wrong with me?" It attacks a person's self-esteem and self-worth. When self-esteem is attacked, especially over a period of time, it takes a negative toll on the person's life and future. It can lead to depression, anger, revenge, thoughts of suicide, and under-achieving. It is easier for many people to believe there is something wrong with them than wrong with society. Being treated as one who is unwelcome – whether the rejection comes from family, school, church, a neighborhood, or a group – has devastating consequences.

God does not create life to destroy it. God does not create life to make it unwelcome. Even when someone is "left out" because of their own choices or behavior, our choice to respond with the lack of hospitality is still unGodly. Somehow, we must ask God to give us His heart. That is how our hearts are ultimately re-formed. We give God our heart and in return, God who is never outdone in generosity, gives us His heart in return. And let me say with absolute certainty that I believe the human spirit is strong enough to transform the hardened heart of an unbeliever so that they seek a new heart and a new set of glasses through which to view the world.

So, since I promised some practical suggestions, let me be so bold as to offer some.

1. Basic human decency and human kindness matter. The simple things our mothers taught us, and that we learned in kindergarten are still true and still valuable. "Thank you", "hello", "I am sorry", "glad to see you" still carry tremendous weight even in our world filled with tweeting and texting.

2. When someone enters your world, your space, or your life, ask yourself the simple question "what might this person need to make their life a little better?" It sounds simple, but if we all tried to make another's life more enjoyable and pleasant, all of us would live in a better world.

3. For a moment in time, put yourself second. Allowing the other to be the center of attention and to feel valued is a precious gift to give another human being. Certainly, our own self-confidence should be strong enough to allow another to be cherished.

4. Don't ever presume that basic human needs (water, food, bathrooms, a seat to rest) are available. A small amount of human compassion speaks volumes. And, a small act of

kindness like a bottle of water can break down the fear of the other person.

5. Listen for names. Calling someone by name has a power in itself. It's not enough to say "I am just bad at remembering names." Make an effort to learn names. And listen carefully, to hear the other person's story. In a few moments, we can gain a tremendous amount of insight into someone else when we simply listen. LISTEN. Be more anxious to hear from someone else than simply to speak your own story or your own thoughts.

6. Say something affirming to another person, even if you don't know the person well. Affirmation is a tremendous way to connect to another human being. Assuming the positive and not the negative about someone is a good place to start with hospitality.

7. Try to see the face of God in the other. Greet others as you would greet Christ. As Christians and as believers, our faith tells us God dwells within His creation. He certainly dwells within His children.

8. Don't judge another person. No matter what you have heard about an individual or a group of people, don't let somebody else make decisions about what your values should me. It is amazing that in this day and time, there are churches and groups that condemn those who are divorced. According to scripture it is never our role to judge another person's heart. Heaven knows, it is often hard enough to keep track of our own hearts. And certainly don't pre-judge someone because of color, culture, or looks. Prejudice is a hideous disease which continues to plague our world, even though we know better.

9. Believe in your own heart that the other person has something to say, something worthwhile to offer. Approach others with confidence that whatever they have to give or to offer is something that will make a difference. Simply by caring about the other, you will make strong statements about human dignity.

10. Do not let yourself become a fear-based person. The world we live in is not always safe, and certainly we must be aware of our world and our surroundings. But being aware and being fear-based are not the same. Fear-based living is a defensive posture. Your fists are always raised in order to protect yourself. Your neck is always tensed up ready to receive a blow. When we live this way, hospitality becomes impossible.

These ten suggestions will make our families and our homes a better place. And certainly, if these things could become an integral part of our churches, they would change the face of religion in our society. If we truly believe that God dwells in another, perhaps we have a chance of convincing someone to believe that God dwells in him or her. And, even in our business world, if we could begin to treat others with kindness and not treat individuals like they are just another number or another phone call, we could change our living environment.

The truth is, each of us has control over one human being. And clearly that person is oneself. The world will always have mean and nasty people residing in it. People who will choose to act badly are born every minute. But, we do not need to give these types of people control over our world. Certainly there will be those who take advantage of the kindness we offer, and of us. But, what options do we have? There are really only two: to live in a tight-fisted, tense, inhospitable world or to live in a world where we assume the positive and we do our best to dignify each person we meet. To me, the second is the better option – and is the option that will change the world.

CHAPTER 9
PERSONAL REFLECTIONS

REV. DALE FUSHEK - JODY SEREY

REV. DALE FUSHEK

In my Polish family, hospitality seems second nature. The door was always open, extended family was always living with us, and food (especially dessert) was always abundant. My friends used to laugh at my mom who would echo the same words every time they came to visit, "Are you going to stay for dinner or not?" (By the way, they usually stayed.)

And for me, going to an aunt's house meant home-made cakes and Polish cookies. These are all great memories and were teaching moments about how to welcome someone to your home. I am sure that many others who were raised in an ethnic or cultural home experienced the same type of training.

At the same time, many of these same relatives were

prejudiced, close-minded, and closed to folks who were different. These things go contrary to the notion of hospitality. You cannot welcome someone you have already judged.

As an adult, and especially as a pastor, I tried my best to be welcoming. As a pastor in the Catholic Church there were always a number of rules and regulations that set boundaries on welcoming others. And, although I did my best to represent the position of the hierarchy, I also did my best to help people to be true to their inner calling from God. For instance, I know many divorced people and non-Catholics received communion. I was always peaceful with that practice even though it was against the law of the Catholic Church.

I believed the church should be a big tent welcoming all. That is how St. Timothy's in Mesa, Arizona, grew so large (8,000 to 10,000 attendees each Sunday). I also knew a lot of folks who were involved didn't agree with all the teachings of the Catholic Church. I always felt that as long as they were there, as long as their hearts were open, my job was to teach them and to call them to a deeper understanding of faith. I chose to always see the positive in others and to believe that having them there was better than them not being there.

After accusations were made against me in 2004, even though they were bizarre and untrue, I came to understand what it meant to be on the other side, the outside. I was given a few hours to leave my home, leave my job, and leave my life. No one – literally no one – cared where I was to go and what my needs were. No one from the church I loved, and the parish that was my family, invited me in for healing or hope. I was told NOT to come on church property, and to stay away from the place (St. Tim's) that I loved so dearly.

As time went on, things got worse. Between a power-leader bishop, an egomaniac county attorney, and a media gone into frenzy, my life was ruined. Eventually, when I made the decision to continue to pray with a group of friends, against the command of the bishop of Phoenix, I was ex-communicated. As a result of this action, I could not pray in Catholic churches or receive the sacraments that Catholics believe are so important for conversion. I am no longer worthy, according to the Catholic hierarchy, to sit with other Christians or to pray to the forgiving and merciful God. I find it very interesting that in his classic book, **People of the Lie**, Scott Peck says "Evil is defined as the use of power to destroy the spiritual growth of others for the purpose of defending and preserving the integrity of our own sick selves." This definition hit very close to home.

Now that all this is behind me, and I am pastor of a very welcoming community, I still hurt deeply at the lack of hospitality from the church to which I had given my life. Priests that I called "brother" turned not only away from me, but on me. Even parishioners who told me they loved me did not know how to help or chose not to get involved. My legal situation ended in a silly $250 fine after five years of legal torment. Maricopa County had spent hundreds of thousands of dollars investigating and prosecuting. Although I am happy this nightmarish time of my life is behind me, the lack of hospitality and compassion still eat away at my heart and my spirit.

Once you have been the victim of an "un-welcoming" institution you become far more sensitive to the plight of others. Businesses that are unkind and un-welcoming are no longer acceptable to me. Politicians who agree with my thoughts but try to destroy others who think differently no longer get my vote. Churches that create barriers to God's love are no longer simply "not cool", but I now see them as destructive. The hardest reality for me to deal with is that the church that I loved so much, and worked so hard to build, is now seen as a destructive force in our contemporary world. Many of my closest friends stayed part of the Catholic Church. They would tell me they thought what happened to me was unfair, but they did not want to stand up to the hierarchy. And, they certainly didn't want to walk away from the faith of their childhood and tradition.

The problem is obvious. When you endorse a church, an organization, or even a company that welcomes YOU but not others, you are buying into a system. The system is used to purify the organization and to keep out the unworthy. But clearly, it will only be a matter of time until you become or one of your family becomes the outsider. If we, as a society, do not stand up for the marginalized, the sinners, the poor, those with different colored skin, those who are politically different, those with a different thought process, it will only be a matter of time before we will be on the outside. The blonde-haired, blue-eyed Germans of World War II were never safely ensconced as members of a superior race. They simply were the power for a short period of history, and that passed away.

I always believed in hospitality as a way of life. My instincts have always turned me away from unfriendly businesses and people. But now, after being the one told there was "no room in the inn," I am absolute in my conviction that hospitality lies at the foundation of all that is truly human and all that is holy. Unwelcoming churches misrepresent God. Unwelcoming educational institutions give learning a bad name. Unwelcoming businesses don't deserve to flourish. An unwelcoming government goes contrary to the very nature of our tradition, history, and our constitution. And unwelcoming people make the world a much darker place.

JODY SEREY

For a few years during my early childhood, we lived in the deep South while my father taught English at a university. My parents were Midwesterners, and were not prepared for the ferocity of the prejudice that was on open display in the 1950s. I sensed the underlying tensions of the time, but was too young and too inexperienced to give them a name. I just knew that there was a lot of fear, and a lot of anger. And it made me feel uneasy all the time.

My mother introduced racial integration to the local girls' camp unintentionally when she went on as camp director for the summer and accepted the application of every girl of every color who applied to attend. There was an initial murmur of disapproval from the townspeople, which she ignored, and camp went on as usual with only one girl being pulled from the roster by indignant parents.

When the second grade class fell through the floor and landed in the basement at the so-called "separate but equal" (but crumbling) grade school in the African American settlement, Mom threw us kids in the back seat of the Plymouth and we rushed over so she could help. I can remember her driving as fast as she dared, and since it was before the era of seatbelts, my little sister and I were warned to "hang tight." We arrived while the dust was still hanging in the air, and frantic mothers were pulling kids out of the debris. Exactly one ambulance arrived, and the rest of the children who were scuffed up and bruised had to be transported however they could be to the local hospital, where my mother said they waited for hours to be seen. Nobody was killed, but my mother was never the same.

One time at a city park, I got thirsty and went to get a drink of water. There were two spigots – one marked "white" and one marked "colored." I thought the signs indicated the color of the water, and decided that I wanted colored water to drink instead of plain, so I turned on the spigot marked "colored." My mother came to check on me, and I complained that the water was still plain, and wasn't colored at all. She said, "It's false advertising. The water all comes from the same pipe. So get a drink wherever the line is the shortest. And if anybody says anything to you, you tell them your mother says you can get a drink wherever you want to. And if she's around, so can any other child." It wasn't until much later that I realized the significance of those labels. And of what my young mother faced down and defied.

Can there by anything more dehumanizing than needing a drink, or food, or the use of a restroom and being verbally abused or denied access to basic necessities? Is there anything less welcoming than not being wanted next to somebody on a bus seat, on an airplane, in a neighborhood, in a church pew?

Whatever sets another apart from the portion of society in power is not of God, but of the ones He created equally and who should read their own refrigerator magnets and bumper stickers. "Encourage one another day after day" makes its way onto plaques across the country, but the chronically mentally ill and the homeless are usually not greeted with much enthusiasm by the public that barely endures their presence. Parents of handicapped children fear for the safety of their sons and daughters when they send them off to school, and anybody wearing a turban in certain cities fears being the victim of a drive-by shooting.

Hospitality is anticipating the needs of another, and taking action to see that a direct request for assistance may not be necessary. Human dignity is sustained, for both the giver and the receiver. Hospitality is both an art and a ministry. A certain understanding of the desperation of the one in need is required of the host, so that the receiver is not reduced to being less than he or she truly is.

Hospitality does not mean driving an SUV alone into the ghetto on Christmas Eve while wearing an expensive watch and a fancy sweater to pass out ham sandwiches. The gesture, although made with the best of intentions by the local business woman who attempted it, did not end well, although she survived. You can't put more weight on a person's vulnerabilities than can be supported under adverse conditions, and the watch, car, and fancy sweater were soon removed from the woman's immediate possession and put to unspecified use elsewhere. In the end, the woman became an embittered "victim" of a crime, and others already coping with hopelessness and diminished circumstances became "thieves."

Fortunately, the angels embrace both saints and sinners, and all of us in between. But that night hospitality encountered a big "fail" instead of becoming the occasion for transformation.

QUESTIONS TO CONSIDER:

Am I a self-centered person, or other-centered person?

Am I willing to do the work it takes to be a hospitable person? And truly welcome someone else into my world?

Can I anticipate the needs of another?

Am I basically a generous person?

Am I okay with focusing attention on someone else and diverting attention away from me?

Did my family teach me the basics of hospitality and kindness?

Do I personally raise barriers to people I don't like?

Do I harbor prejudice in me? Am I fearful of people who look or think in different ways than I do?

Do I listen to others? Do I do more talking than I should?

Do I see God in the face of others? Am I open to entertaining angels by entertaining strangers?

Is hospitality a spiritual experience for me?

CHAPTER 10
A FINAL REFLECTION

JODY SEREY

Hospitality requires acceptance of the stranger, and the willingness to suspend judgment. We can expand our definition of hospitality to also include non-human living beings, and experiences we encounter unexpectedly. If we welcome wonder into our midst, it can arrive in almost any form and leave its gifts with us forever.

In the 1950s in Arkansas it was safe to walk home alone from school. I loved the four-block journey at the end of the day, and once in awhile I found something interesting to take home to my mother. Rocks and autumn leaves were standard offerings. However, one cool afternoon I found an enormous green caterpillar crawling in the middle of the sidewalk.

At first I was afraid to touch him. Feathered and fancy and covered with bumps, he was the most complicated caterpillar

I had ever seen. A system of brightly colored dots and designs covered his entire length. I was awestruck, but worried. The neighborhood was filled kids and cars that could make short work of him.

So I picked him up. He immediately twisted in my hand, and the bumps and feathers poked my palm. Startled, I dropped him. He fell to the ground, lay still, then righted himself with a backwards somersault and crawled towards me in a surprisingly fast series of foldings and unfoldings. In an instant he had fixed himself to the ankle of my red knee sock. Unwilling to risk hurting him by prying him off, I decided to get my mother to help me.

I went home and limped into the back bedroom where she usually could be found. As I expected, my mother was sitting at her typewriter working on a stack of papers and manuscripts. Her typing and editing service added to my father's teaching salary, and she always seemed to be very busy. She had explained many times that it was a time consuming and difficult task to produce pages of perfect typewritten text, each piece of paper unbroken by even a single erasure. Most of the time I tried to keep from bothering her. However, today I stood in back of her and waited for her to look up.

My mother turned from her work. "Did you get hurt?" she asked.

"No," I answered. "There's a caterpillar on my knee sock."

"Well, look at that," said Mom. "He's a big one. Why don't you get him some leaves and a stick and put him in something?"

"Okay, if you'll take him off."

She got him loose, and I spent the entire evening with my nose against the side of a peanut butter jar that I had pressed into service as a caterpillar refuge. When I turned off the light to go to sleep that night, I promised him, "Don't worry. I'll let you go in the morning."

When the sun came up, I jumped out of bed and ran to check on him. However, he was nowhere to be seen. At the bottom of the jar attached to the stick was a dark green lump that in no way resembled my magnificent find of the day before. The caterpillar seemed to have vanished without a trace. I ran into the back bedroom. My mother was already up and hard at work, sitting at her typewriter.

"What's wrong?" she asked.

"He's gone," I said, adding a dramatic sigh to the end of my two-word statement.

"Who's gone?"

"The caterpillar!"

Mom smiled. "No, he's still in there. I checked on him myself. You just don't recognize him."

"What do you mean?" I asked.

"He's in there working on something," she continued, "but it will take awhile."

"He's inside that lump?" I asked.

"He is that lump," she assured me.

So the peanut butter jar and its contents took up residence on a windowsill in the back bedroom where it sat in the sun away from the reach of the baby and the cat.

For awhile I visited it frequently, then as the days passed by I thought about the caterpillar less and less. Despite my mother's assurances that he was in there working on something, he didn't seem to be doing anything at all. The lump never moved, and never seemed to change. It just sat there silently in the bottom of the jar, and absorbed the light and the sound of my mother's typewriter. Occasionally, I picked up the jar and shook it gently, but the dry rattle revealed nothing. Eventually, I ceased to notice the jar at all.

As the fall sped towards Christmas, I prayed for snow -- an unlikely occurrence in that part of Arkansas. This year was no different. In fact, instead of hurling ourselves into holiday drifts, we plunged into a balmy warm spell that sent the birds hopping across the yard, and the children outside without sweaters. I was thoroughly disgusted, and stenciled icicles on the windows in an attempt to add a little winter wonderland atmosphere to an otherwise tropical holiday season.

School was almost out for Christmas vacation, and I sweated my way through the pageant at school, my crepe paper Frosty the Snowman costume limp and damp. My mother typed day and night, trying to finish up all the term papers the local college students brought her to complete before the end of the term. I tried to pretend that the clacking of the typewriter keys was the "prancing and pawing of each little hoof," but my summer pajamas and the presence of the window fan spoiled the illusion.

My dreams for Christmas were as tattered as the old red bow on the wreath my father hung on the front door. "Why don't we get a new one?" I asked him.

He seemed surprised. "I've put this on door every year since your mother and I got married. It's a tradition."

However, one tradition was sidelined that year. My mother had too much work to do her usual baking, so Dad bought the holiday cookies at the grocery store. I licked the frosting off a gingerbread reindeer and scowled.

That night, I pulled the sheet up over my head and went to sleep to dream of sleigh rides and things I would never see in Fayetteville. Much later, I woke up to my mother's whisper. "You've got to get up, honey. There's something you have to see."

Certain that Santa had stumbled down our chimney a couple of days early, I followed down the hall behind my mother and into the back bedroom. My father was waiting for me too, his eyes excited.

I peered around, looking for a Christmas miracle. Finding nothing, I asked, "What's happening?"

My father said, "Your caterpillar finished changing into a butterfly. Actually, he changed into a cecropia moth. But he's going to be a beauty."

I followed his gaze towards one of the manuscript boxes my mother used to place finished pages, expecting to see a brightly colored pair of wings. Instead, a little wet creature crawled from manuscript box to manuscript box, soaking through original pages and carbon copies alike. I was indignant. "He's ugly!"

"Just wait," my mother said. "He's not finished."

I sat down between my parents, and watched the newly hatched moth move his wings for the first time, then gradually straighten himself out. The entire time, he walked back and forth over the neat boxes of typed manuscripts, and even I knew that my mother faced hours of additional work to replace the pages that the moth spoiled and left damp. But she didn't seem to mind and smiled at him as he dried off, his wings beginning to show their colors. I saw how happy she seemed, despite having little sleep in many days. I moved closer to her on the bed.

The sun came up, and the moth warmed himself on the windowsill, slowly fanning his wings and moving his legs. My father remarked, "He's lucky it's so warm. It's the wrong time of year for moths and butterflies."

I thought, it's winter! It's Christmas!

I was suddenly alarmed. "What will happen to him?"

My mother said, "He doesn't need much time to get his work done. So as long as this warm weather holds he'll be okay. But we've got to let him go. He can't do anything locked up in the house."

So after the sun was high and the morning mild and sunny, we took the moth outside perched on the end of a stick. He paused for awhile, then fluttered without a sound up into the naked maple tree and rested.

I cupped my hands around my eyes and watched him as he

paused, a single ornament in the dark branches. Then silently he flew away, flashing bright as a memory.

KINDNESS MATTERS: HOSPITALITY IN A HOSTILE WORLD

www.ingramcontent.com/pod-product-compliance
Lightning Source LLC
Chambersburg PA
CBHW051849040426
42447CB00006B/766